D1495387

Singing Words

Singing Words

Poems Selected

By

Alice G. Thorn

Illustrated by
MASHA

Granger Index Reprint Series

BOOKS FOR LIBRARIES PRESS
FREEPORT, NEW YORK

INTERNATIONAL STANDARD BOOK NUMBER:
0-8369-6337-7

LIBRARY OF CONGRESS CATALOG CARD NUMBER:
79-38605

PRINTED IN THE UNITED STATES OF AMERICA
BY
NEW WORLD BOOK MANUFACTURING CO., INC.
HALLANDALE, FLORIDA 33009

For Children Who Read This Book

When rhymes and jingles are spoken, their dancing measures
—now short and long, now soft then loud, now tumbling over and
over—all these gay patterns of words begin to "sing themselves."
As we keep repeating them, tones begin to dance along with the
words and the words blend into the music. When we begin a
counting out rhyme and say the numbers over and over again, we
find that we are singing as we count. Even poems, perhaps a little
more dignified than jingles, have a swinging rhythmic sound
which sometimes turns into music as we say them.

Since music and poetry are such good friends we have invited
six songs to be in this book of poems. The poems are divided
into six groups and there is a song at the beginning of each group.
You will find music hiding in many of the other words, too. It is
only waiting for you to say the poems you like best over and over
again. Then you will hear the music in them!

Alice G. Thorn

ACKNOWLEDGMENTS

Grateful acknowledgment is made to the following publishers and authors for permission to use poems and music included in this book.

Doubleday, Doran and Co., for *Taxis,* and *General Store* from TAXIS AND TOADSTOOLS by Rachel Field.

Frederick Stokes and Co., for *The Wires Are So Still and High, Indian Children,* and *Once When We Were Walking* from FOR DAYS AND DAYS by Annette Wynne. Also for *After Tea, A Kitten,* and *City Streets and Country Roads* from OVER THE GARDEN WALL and JOAN'S DOOR by Eleanor Farjeon.

The Macmillan Co., for *The Lost Bell* from BRANCHES GREEN, and *Seven Ages of Elf-hood* from ELIZA AND THE ELVES, both by Rachel Field. Also for *Things Left Alone* from SKIPPING ALONG ALONE by Winifred Welles.`

Charles Scribner's Sons for *Ducks' Ditty* from THE WIND IN THE WILLOWS by Kenneth Grahame.

Harper and Bros. for *I Want a Pony* from COUNTING THE DAYS by James S. Tippett.

The Viking Press for *Firefly* from UNDER THE TREE by Elizabeth Madox Roberts.

Little, Brown and Co., for *The Mermaidens,* and *Eletelephony* from TIRRA LIRRA by Laura Richards.

The Incorporated Society of Authors, Playwrights and Composers for *Singing Time,* and *The Fairy Flute* from THE FAIRY FLUTE by Rose Fyleman. John Day for the music of *Singing* from SINGING TIME by Satis Coleman and Alice G. Thorn.

Jack and Jill magazine and to Barbara Jones for *The Tree Comes Down.*

Henry Holt and Co. for *Some One* by Walter de la Mare from POEMS FOR CHILDREN.

Ruth Hilliard for the words of *Spring and Summer* from ONE AND TWENTY SONGS by Corinne Brown.

E. C. Schirmer Music Co. for the words and music of *Gingerbread Lady* from A KINDERGARTEN BOOK OF FOLK SONGS by Lorraine d'O. Warner.

Eleanor Smith for the words and music of *Bossy Cow* from SONGS OF A LITTLE CHILD'S DAY by Emilie Poulsson and Eleanor Smith.

Ginn and Co., for the words and music of *Christmas Eve* from SING A SONG OF THE WORLD OF MUSIC.

TABLE OF CONTENTS FOR SINGING WORDS

EVERY-DAY DOINGS

Singing Time

ROSE FYLEMAN

ALICE G. THORN

I wake in the morn - ing ear - ly, and
al - ways the ve - ry first thing, I poke out my head and I
sit up in bed, and I sing and I 'sing and I sing!

Taxis

Ho, for taxis green or blue,
  Hi, for taxis red,
They roll along the Avenue
  Like spools of colored thread!

  Jack-o'-Lantern yellow,
  Orange as the moon,
  Greener than the greenest grass
  Ever grew in June.

  Gaily striped or checked in squares,
  Wheels that twinkle bright,
  Don't you think that taxis make
  A very pleasant sight?

  Taxis shiny in the rain,
  Scudding through the snow,
  Taxis flashing back the sun.
  Waiting in a row.

Ho, for taxis red and green,
  Hi, for taxis blue,
I wouldn't be a private car
  In sober black, would you?

Rachel Field

My Ship and I

O it's I that am the captain of a tidy little ship,
    Of a ship that goes a-sailing on the pond;
And my ship it keeps a-turning all around and all about;
But when I'm a little older, I shall find the secret out
    How to send my vessel sailing on beyond.

For I mean to grow as little as the dolly at the helm,
    And the dolly I intend to come alive;
And with him beside to help me, it's a-sailing I shall go,
It's a-sailing on the water, when the jolly breezes blow
    And the vessel goes a divie-divie-dive.

O it's then you'll see me sailing through the rushes
        and the reeds.
    And you'll hear the water singing at the prow;
For beside the dolly sailor, I'm to voyage and explore,
To land upon the island where no dolly was before,
    And to fire the penny cannon in the bow.

Robert Louis Stevenson

A Swing Song

Swing, swing,
Sing, sing,
Here! my throne and I am a King!
Swing, sing,
Swing, sing,
Farewell, earth, for I'm on the wing!

Low, high,
Here I fly,
Like a bird through sunny sky:
Free, free,
Over the lea,
Over the mountain, over the sea!

Up, down,
Up and down,
Which is the way to London Town?
Where? Where?
Up in the air,
Close your eyes, and now you are there!

Soon, soon,
Afternoon,
Over the sunset, over the moon:
Far, far,
Over all bar,
Sweeping on from star to star!

No, no,
Low, low,
Sweeping daisies with my toe.
Slow, slow,
To and fro,
Slow—
    slow—
       slow—
          slow.

William Allingham

General Store

Some day I'm going to have a store
With a tinkly bell hung over the door,
With real glass cases and counters wide
And drawers all spilly with things inside.
There'll be a little of everything:
Bolts of calico; balls of string;
Jars of peppermint; tins of tea;
Pots and kettles and crockery;
Seeds in packets; scissors bright;
Kegs of sugar, brown and white;
Sarsaparilla for picnic lunches,
Bananas and rubber boots in bunches.
I'll fix the window and dust each shelf,
And take the money in all myself.
It will be my store and I will say:
"What can I do for you today?"

Rachel Field

Indian Children

Where we walk to school each day
Indian children used to play—
All about our native land,
Where the shops and houses stand.

And the trees were very tall,
And there were no streets at all,
Not a church and not a steeple—
Only woods and Indian people.

Only wigwams on the ground,
And at night bears prowling round—
What a different place today
Where we live and work and play!

Annette Wynne

An Indian Lullaby

Rock-a-by, rock-a-by, little brown baby,
  Safe in the green branch so high,
Shut your bright black eyes and go to sleep, baby,
  While the wood-wind sings, "Hush-a-by-by."

"Hush-a-by-hush," 'tis the voice of the forest,
  "Hush-a-by-hush," the leaves seem to say,
"Hush-a-by-hush," sing the wild birds in chorus
  Up in the tree-tops so far, far away.

Rock-a-by, rock-a-by, swinging so gently,
  See, from the dark woods so cool and so deep,
The little gray squirrel, the timid brown rabbit,
  Are coming to see if papoose is asleep.

Mother will watch by her little brown baby,
  Swinging aloft on the green branch so high,
No harm can come to the little brown baby,
  Hush-a-by, rock-a-by, hush-a-by-by.

Anonymous

After Tea

Listen! that's Mother singing and playing.
    Oh, what a lovely chance!
The lights are down and the shadows are swaying,
    Let us go sing and dance.

She'll smile at us, but she won't stop singing
    The sweetest tunes she knows.
In the far corners the shadows are swinging,
    The fire on the ceiling glows.

Nobody plays such music as Mother.
    She plays it for me and you.
The shadows are dancing with one another—
    Let us start dancing too.

Eleanor Farjeon

OUT-OF-DOORS

Spring and Summer

CORINNE BROWN

Spring-time, flow- er time, daf-fo-dils and dais-ies! South-winds
June-time, sum-mer time, morn-ing glo-ries nod-ding! Ros - es

blow-ing will the blos-soms bring, Rope-time, mar-ble time,
blow-ing and the pans-ies gay, Kite-time, pic-nic time,

Time to go a May-ing, What so pleas-ant as a day in Spring?
Time to go a wad-ing, What so pleas-ant as a Sum-mer day?

The Months

January brings the snow,
Makes our feet and fingers glow.

February brings the rain,
Thaws the frozen lake again.

March brings breezes loud and shrill,
Stirs the dancing daffodil.

April brings the primrose sweet,
Scatters daisies at our feet.

May brings flocks of pretty lambs,
Skipping by their fleecy dams.

June brings tulips, lilies, roses,
Fills the children's hands with posies.

Hot July brings cooling showers,
Apricots and gillyflowers.

August brings the sheaves of corn,
Then the harvest home is borne.

Warm September brings the fruit,
Sportsmen then begin to shoot.

Fresh October brings the pheasant,
Then to gather nuts is pleasant.

Dull November brings the blast,
Then the leaves are whirling fast.

Chill December brings the sleet,
Blazing fire and Christmas treat.

Sara Coleridge

Growing in the Vale

Growing in the vale
 By the uplands hilly,
Growing straight and frail,
 Lady Daffadowndilly.

In a golden crown,
And a scant green gown
 While the spring blows chilly,
Lady Daffadown,
 Sweet Daffadowndilly.

Daisies

Where innocent bright-eyed daisies are,
 With blades of grass between.
Each daisy stands up like a star
 Out of a sky of green.

Christina G. Rossetti

Winter Night

Blow, wind, blow!
Drift the flying snow!
Send it twirling, whirling overhead!
There, bedroom in a tree
Where, snug as snug can be,
The squirrel nests in his cosy bed.

Shriek, wind, shriek!
Make the branches creak!
Battle with the boughs till break o' day!
In a snow-cave warm and tight,
Through the icy winter night
The rabbit sleeps the peaceful hours away.

Call, wind, call,
In entry and in hall,
Straight from off the mountain white and wild!
Soft purrs the pussy-cat,
On her little fluffy mat,
And beside her nestles close her furry child.

Scold, wind, scold,
So bitter and so bold!
Shake the windows with your tap, tap, tap!
With half-shut, dreamy eyes
The drowsy baby lies
Cuddled closely in his mother's lap.

Mary Frances Butts

Who Likes the Rain?

"I," said the duck. "I call it fun,
For I have my pretty red rubbers on;
They make a little three-toed track,
In the soft, cool mud,—quack, quack!"

"I!" cried the dandelion, "I!
My roots are thirsty, my buds are dry."
And she lifted a towsled yellow head
Out of her green and grassy bed.

"I hope 'twill pour! I hope 'twill pour!"
Croaked the tree-toad from his gray bark door,
"For, with a broad leaf for a roof,
I'm always safely weather-proof."

Sang the brook: "I laugh at every drop,
Come down, dear raindrops, never stop
Until a broad river you make of me,
And then I will carry you to the sea."

Clara Doty Bates

Sea Shell

Sea Shell, Sea Shell,
  Sing me a song, O please!
A song of ships, and sailor men,
  And parrots, and tropical trees,

Of islands lost in the Spanish Main
Which no man ever may find again,
Of fishes and corals under the waves,
And sea-horses stabled in great green caves.

Sea Shell, Sea Shell,
Sing of the things you know so well.

Amy Lowell

Who Has Seen the Wind?

Who has seen the wind?
 Neither I nor you;
But when the leaves hang trembling,
 The wind is passing thro'.

Who has seen the wind?
 Neither you nor I;
But when the trees bow down their heads,
 The wind is passing by.

Christina G. Rossetti

City Streets and Country Roads

The city has streets—
 But the country has roads.
In the country one meets
 Blue carts with their loads
Of sweet-smelling hay,
 And mangolds, and grain:
Oh, take me away
 To the country again!

Eleanor Farjeon

Apple Song

The apples are seasoned
And ripe and sound.
Gently they fall
On the yellow ground.

The apples are stored
In the dusky bin
Where hardly a glimmer
Of light creeps in.

In the firelit, winter
Nights, they'll be
The clear sweet taste
Of a summer tree!

Frances Frost

The Wires Are So Still and High

The wires are so still and high
We never hear the words go by,
Yet messages fly far and near—
I wonder if the birds can hear.

And when they perch on wires and sing,
I wonder are they listening,
And telling out to earth and sky
A lovely word is going by!

Annette Wynne

ANIMAL FRIENDS

Bossy Cow

EMILIE POULSSON

ELEANOR SMITH

Ting ting tin-kle, ting, Tin-kle, ting a - gain.
Good old bos-sy cow What does Bos-sy bring?

Here comes Bos-sy cow Stroll-ing down the lane.
Fresh milk for us all, Tin-kle, tin-kle, ting.

The Squirrel

Whisky, frisky,
Hippity hop,
Up he goes
To the tree top!

Whirly, twirly,
Round and round,
Down he scampers
To the ground.

Furly, curly,
What a tail!
Tall as a feather,
Broad as a sail!

Where's his supper?
In the shell,
Snappity, crackity,
Out it fell.

Author Unknown

Ducks' Ditty

All along the backwater,
Through the rushes tall,
Ducks are a-dabbling,
Up tails all!

Ducks' tails, drakes' tails,
Yellow feet a-quiver,
Yellow bills all out of sight
Busy in the river!

Slushy green undergrowth
Where the roach swim—
Here we keep our larder,
Cool and full and dim.

Everyone for what he likes!
WE like to be
Heads down, tails up,
Dabbling free!

High in the blue above
Swifts whirl and call—
WE are down a-dabbling,
Up tails all!

Kenneth Grahame

On the Grassy Banks

On the grassy banks
Lambkins at their pranks;
Wooly sisters, wooly brothers
Jumping off their feet,
While their wooly mothers
Watch by them and bleat.

Christina Rossetti

A Kitten

He's nothing much but fur
And two round eyes of blue,
He has a giant purr
And a midget mew.

He darts and pats the air,
He starts and cocks his ear,
When there is nothing there
For him to see and hear.

Eleanor Farjeon

The Lost Bell

My dog Trot
Has lost her bell.
Where it rings now
Who can tell?
By berry bramble,
And juniper,
Where grass grows thick
As soft green fur;
Where rabbits scuttle,
And chipmunks scold,
Where sunlight wavers
Through branches old;
From thorny thicket,
And mossy ground,
Have you heard a bell
With a silver sound?
In weedy rock-pool
With sea flung shell,—
Wherever she left it
Trot won't tell!

Rachel Field

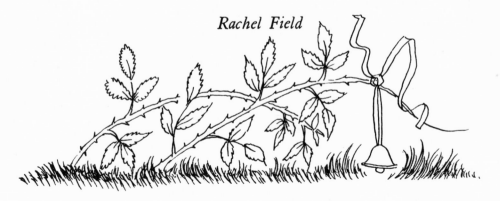

I Want a Pony

I want a dappled pony,
I'll ride him far away
Across the hills and valleys
Through blossomings of May.

I want a coal black pony,
Neither mild nor shy,
To carry me through shady lanes
In sweltering July.

I want a small brown pony,
He must not be too sober,
We'll race along the windy roads
In brightly dressed October.

I want a snow white pony,
His color please remember,
To pull a sleigh on snowy days
In shivering December.

I do so want a pony,
Just any kind at all,
To ride in spring and summer,
In winter and in fall.

James Tippett

Firefly

(A SONG)

A little light is going by,
Is going up to see the sky,
A little light with wings.

I never could have thought of it,
To have a little bug all lit
And made to go on wings.

Elizabeth Madox Roberts

Although the night is dark
The little firefly ventures out,
And slowly lights his lamp.

Traditional (Japanese)

SPECIAL DAYS

Christmas Eve

MARY SMITH   Swedish Folk Tune

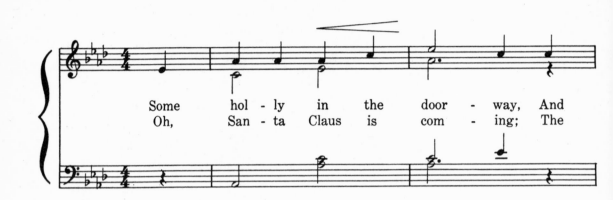

Some   hol - ly   in   the   door - way,   And
Oh,   San - ta   Claus   is   com - ing;   The

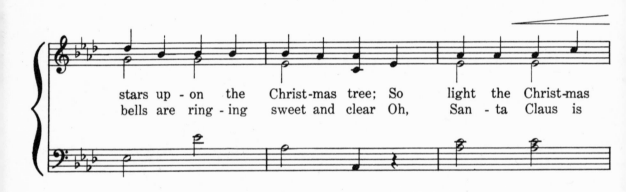

stars up - on   the   Christ-mas tree; So   light   the Christ-mas
bells are ring - ing   sweet and clear Oh,   San - ta   Claus is

can - dles   For   San - ta   Claus to   see.
com - ing,   For   Christ-mas Eve   is   here!

Cradle Hymn

Away in a manger,
No crib for a bed,
The little Lord Jesus
Lay down his sweet head;
The stars in the heavens
Looked down where he lay,
The little Lord Jesus
Asleep in the hay.

The cattle are lowing,
The poor baby wakes,
But little Lord Jesus
No crying he makes.
I love thee, Lord Jesus,
Look down from the sky,
And stay by my cradle
Till morning is nigh.

Martin Luther

Christmas Song

Why do bells for Christmas ring?
Why do little children sing?

Once a lovely, shining star,
Seen by shepherds from afar,
Gently moved until its light
Made a manger-cradle bright.
There a darling baby lay
Pillowed soft upon the hay.
And his mother sang and smiled,
"This is Christ, the holy child."

So the bells for Christmas ring.
So the little children sing.

Lydia Avery Coonley Ward

The Friendly Beasts

Jesus our brother, strong and good,
Was humbly born in a stable rude,
And the friendly beasts around Him stood,
Jesus our brother, strong and good.

I, said the donkey shaggy and brown,
I carried His mother up hill and down,
I carried her safely to Bethlehem town;
I, said the donkey shaggy and brown.

I, said the cow all white and red,
I gave Him my manger for His bed,
I gave Him my hay to pillow His head;
I, said the cow all white and red.

I, said the sheep with curly horn,
I gave Him my wool for His blanket warm,
He wore my coat on Christmas morn;
I, said the sheep with curly horn.

I, said the dove, from the rafters high,
Cooed Him to sleep that He should not cry.
We cooed Him to sleep, my mate and I;
I, said the dove, from the rafters high.

And every beast, by some good spell,
In the stable dark was glad to tell
Of the gift he gave Immanuel;
The gift he gave Immanuel.

Twelfth Century Carol

Christmas Hearth Rhyme

Sing we all merrily
   Christmas is here,
The day we love best
   Of all days in the year.

Bring forth the holly,
   The box and the bay,
Deck out our cottage
   For glad Christmas day.

Sing we all merrily,
   Draw near the fire,
Sister and brother,
   Grandson and sire.

Old English

The Tree Comes Down

Now, in this box, with tenderness,
Go church and tree and shepherdess.

And into this (oh, wrap them well!)
Each icicle and silver bell.

And carefully, with reverence,
Go tinsel, balls and picket fence.

Oh, place them gently, knowing then,
That Christmas Eve will come again.

Barbara A. Jones

We Thank Thee

For flowers that bloom about our feet;
For tender grass, so fresh, so sweet;
For song of bird, and hum of bee;
For all things fair we hear or see,
    Father in heaven, we thank Thee.

For blue of stream and blue of sky;
For pleasant shade of branches high;
For fragrant air and cooling breeze;
For beauty of the blooming trees,
    Father in heaven, we thank Thee.

Ralph Waldo Emerson

THE FAIRIES

The Fairy Flute

Words by ROSE FYLEMAN

Music by ALICE G. THORN

My broth-er has a lit-tle flute Of gold and i-vor-
He plays it in the mead-ow And eve-ry where he

y. He found it on a sun-ny day With-in a hol-low
walks. The flow-ers start a-nod-ding And a-danc-ing on their

tree. He plays it in the morn-ing And in the af-ter-
stalks, And none but he can hear it And none can un-der-

noon, And all the lit-tle sing-ing birds Lis-ten to the tune.
stand Be-cause it is a fair-y flute And came from fair-y-land.

Queen Mab

A little fairy comes at night;
   Her eyes are blue, her hair is brown,
With silver spots upon her wings,
   And from the moon she flutters down.

She has a little silver wand,
   And when a good child goes to bed,
She waves her wand from right to left,
   And makes a circle round its head.

And then it dreams of pleasant things—
   Of fountains filled with fairy fish,
And trees that bear delicious fruit,
   And bow their branches at a wish;

Of arbors filled with dainty scents
   From lovely flowers that never fade,
Bright flies that glitter in the sun,
   And glow-worms shining in the shade;

And talking birds with gifted tongues
   For singing songs and telling tales,
And pretty dwarfs to show the way
   Through fairy hills and fairy dales.

Thomas Hood

The Seven Ages of Elf-hood

When an Elf is as old as a year and a minute
He can wear a cap with a feather in it.

By the time that he is two times two
He has a buckle for either shoe.

At twenty he is fine as a fiddle,
With a little brown belt to go round his middle.

When he's lived for fifty years or so
His coat may have buttons all in a row.

If past three score and ten he's grown,
Two pockets he has for his very own.

At eighty-two or three years old
They bulge and jingle with bits of gold.

But when he's a hundred and a day
He gets a little pipe to play!

Rachel Field

Once When You Were Walking

Once when you were walking across the
 meadow grass,
A little fairy touched you—but you
 never saw her pass.

One day when you were sitting upon a
 mossy stone,
A fairy sat beside you, but you thought
 you were alone.

So no matter what you do, no matter
 where you go,
A fairy may be near you—but you may
 never know.

Annette Wynne

The Mermaidens

The little white mermaidens live in the sea,
In a palace of silver and gold:
And their neat little tails are all covered with scales,
Most beautiful for to behold.

On wild white horses they ride, they ride,
And in chairs of pink coral they sit;
They swim all the night, with a smile of delight,
And never feel tired a bit.

Laura Richards

Horses of the Sea

The horses of the sea
   Rear a foaming crest,
But the horses of the land
   Serve us the best.

The horses of the land
   Munch corn and clover,
While the foaming sea-horses
   Toss and turn over.

Christina G. Rossetti

Some One

Some one came knocking
    At my wee, small door;
Some one came knocking,
    I'm sure—sure—sure;
I listened, I opened,
    I looked to left and right,
But nought there was a-stirring
    In the still dark night;
Only the busy beetle
    Tap-tapping in the wall,
Only from the forest
    The screech-owl's call,
Only the cricket whistling
    While the dewdrops fall,
So I know not who came knocking,
    At all, at all, at all.

Walter de la Mare

JUST FOR FUN

The Gingerbread Lady

English version by L. d'O. W.

French Folk Song
Arranged by J.B. Wekerlin

Once there liv'd a gin-ger-bread la-dy, In a

house of but-ter so sweet, All the walls were lay-er cake

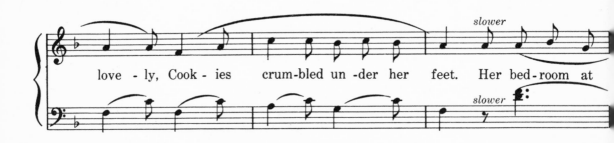

love-ly, Cook-ies crum-bled un-der her feet. Her bed-room at

night With can-dy was bright, Her bed was a bun, Her life was all fun!

Eletelephony

Once there was an elephant,
Who tried to use the telephant—
No! no! I mean an elephone
Who tried to use the telephone—
(Dear me! I am not certain quite
That even now I've got it right.)

Howe'er it was, he got his trunk
Entangled in the telephunk;
The more he tried to get it free,
The louder buzzed the telephee—
(I fear I'd better drop the song
Of elephop and telephong!)

Laura Richards

Nonsense Rhymes

There was an Old Man with a beard,
Who said, "It is just as I feared!—
    Two Owls and a Hen,
    Four Larks and a Wren
Have all built their nests in my beard."

There was a Young Lady of Bute
Who played on a silver-gilt flute.
    She played several jigs
    To her uncle's white pigs,
That amusing Young Lady of Bute.

There was an old person of Ware
Who rode on the back of a bear;
    When they asked, "Does it trot?"
    He said, "Certainly not,
He's a Moppsikon Floppsikon bear!"

Edward Lear

A Farmer Went Trotting

A farmer went trotting
  Upon his gray mare;
Bumpety, bumpety, bump!
With his daughter behind him,
  So rosy and fair;
Lumpety, lumpety, lump!

A raven cried "Croak";
  And they all tumbled down;
Bumpety, bumpety, bump!
The mare broke her knees,
  And the farmer his crown;
Lumpety, lumpety, lump.

The mischievous raven
  Flew laughing away:
Bumpety, bumpety, bump!
And vowed he would serve them
  The same the next day;
Bumpety, bumpety, bump!

Traditional

There Was a Little Girl

There was a little girl, who had a little curl
   Right in the middle of her forehead,
And when she was good, she was very, very good,
   But when she was bad she was horrid.

She stood on her head, on her little trundle-bed,
   With nobody by for to hinder;
She screamed and she squalled, she yelled and she bawled,
   And drummed her little heels against the winder.

Her mother heard the noise, and thought it was the boys
   Playing in the empty attic.
She rushed upstairs, and caught her unawares,
   And spanked her most emphatic.

Henry Wadsworth Longfellow

Things Left Alone

What do the chairs say when we are gone?
　　What does the table do all alone?
Do the sofa cushions leap to the floor,
　　And giggle and dance a jig together?
　　Do the books and lamps run hither and thither?
And squint through the windows and scratch on the door?

When we go back to our house in the dark,
　　Something gives warning, hushes, says, "Hark,
Here THEY are home again!" When we step in,
　　I know that the plates in the pantry smother
　　A little laugh, and, nudging each other,
The dishes keep mum as to where they have been.

Winifred Welles

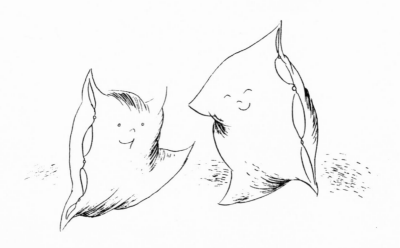

Once There Was a Snowman

Once there was a snowman
   Who stood outside the door.
He wished that he could come inside
   And run about the floor.
He wished that he could warm himself
   Beside the fire, so red.
He wished that he could climb
   Upon the big white bed.

So he called to the North Wind
   "Come and help me, pray,
For I'm completely frozen
   Standing out here all day."
So the North Wind came along
   And blew him in the door
And now there's nothing left of him
   But a puddle on the floor!

Unknown